SILENCE
IS A FOUR-LETTER WORD

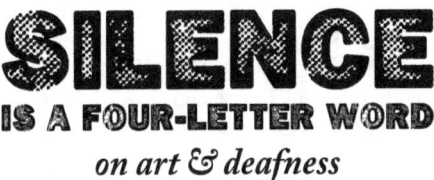

SILENCE
IS A FOUR-LETTER WORD
on art & deafness

RAYMOND LUCZAK

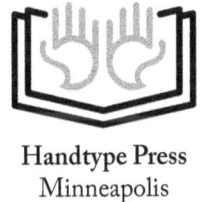

Handtype Press
Minneapolis

ACKNOWLEDGMENTS

The book incorporates excerpts from the following pieces. "Dear Mr. Penn" appeared in *Clerc Scar*. "In the Blink of Dreams" appeared in Tamarind Art Gallery's book for *Sonic Chromatic: Deaf & Hard of Hearing Artists Show 2009*. "Why ASL Storytellers Rule" appeared in the program book for *Tellabration! 2011: A World of Stories*, presented by Northstar Storytelling.

Thanks go to Bryan Borland, David Cummer, Mario Hernandez, Daniel Hochard, Kevin Luczak, Timothy Murphy, Neenyah Ostrom, André Pellerin, Clayton Valli *(in memoriam)*, and Phillip Ward. An endless bouquet of thanks goes to Tom Steele for his continued faith in me. I am forever indebted to Adrean Clark and John Lee Clark for bringing out this book in 2002.

COPYRIGHT

This book is
for deaf artists everywhere.

What follows is a hodgepodge of notes on being a deaf artist, or what I hope to be as an artist. I had been prompted because I kept thinking of how much time I could've saved if I'd read such notes when I was younger, worrying about my future as a deaf gay writer. I didn't know where to go then, except to go to college, and I knew I desperately needed guidance. I needed reassurance that being very different as a writer was indeed all right. I remembered all these feelings when I saw the shining hopeful faces of young deaf writers I'd given a speech to before the winners of the 1998 MacDougall Creative Writing and Evans Journalism Awards at Gallaudet University were announced. What little they knew, and how much they knew! I wanted somehow to say, Here is what I've learned so far.

This book, I hope, will guide deaf people—actually, anyone who feels different for whatever reason—who feel themselves blessed with the impulse to create. Each artist grows and matures, so some advice and opinions dispensed here and there may not be appropriate for you—yet. The bottom line is to get you thinking about what art means to you, and how it could enrich your life. If art should challenge, as it should, I hope you will feel provoked by what I have to say in the pages ahead. Things I once believed in, I sometimes find, may not apply anymore, but the greatest gift in being an artist is the never-ending process of changing and evolving and rediscovering, and leaving behind a record of lessons learned. This is such a record.

That said, take from these pages what moves you now. And do come back when you're older and wiser; take the rest of what moves you then. Only in disagreeing thoughtfully and passionately can you find a sudden agreement within yourself and your art.

1

The urge to create art and tell stories is deep in our bones. It most likely comes from the days when our earliest ancestors had to make do with hand-hewn stone tools and the nights when they huddled around the fire. In that uncertainty of flickering shadows they had to figure out the world around us. It didn't matter whether their stories were fact or fiction; they had to *make sense* and guide their ways. The certainty of these legends was far preferable to the uncertain terrain they had to navigate for food and shelter.

So it is with deaf people. We are constantly creating our own mythologies.

2

Even if you don't know the language, American Sign Language (ASL) is powerful. That alone is a huge reason why many hearing people have constantly tried to ban its use in educational programs for deaf people for decades. It's truly ironic that hearing parents want to learn ASL so they can teach their hearing babies to communicate long before they are able to speak; it's been shown to improve their language acquisition. Yet deaf babies implanted with cochlear implants are often denied this very same opportunity to learn ASL in the belief that *hearing anything* is far more important than communicating in an accessible mode. Sound isn't required for language acquisition. This fact is what hearing parents of deaf children never hear from audiologists and experts. We deaf people know this, but not enough people listen to us. Even with perfect hearing, they do not know how to listen.

But we deaf artists are perhaps the best listeners of them all.

As a deaf artist, you must've asked: What is art? What qualifies deaf art as such? Or Deaf art, with a capitalized "D"? (In this book I make no distinction between the deaf oral and signing communities.)

Some people may say that ASL must be part of the artwork. Others may say that depicting the impact of hearing loss is essential. And a few might venture to say that the hatred of speech therapy is a prerequisite for deaf art. The list of possible criteria for deaf art—or any kind of art, for that matter—is endless. Which is the way it should be.

My answer to the question of deaf art is this: Don't even answer it. I repeat, refuse to answer it. Don't even try. Because true art renders all labels moot ("mute"?). If a work of deaf art is great, it will touch anyone who doesn't know a whit about deaf culture. If a work of art requires a detailed explanation, something's very seriously wrong. It needs to reach us on some gut level; make us react, reflect. If we are strong enough to explore the work in the eye, we may find layers in which we recognize ourselves with a clarity that artists can only provide.

4

When I talk about art, I'm not talking about masterly painting or a well-written book.

Art is more a state of mind that transcends craft.

Art is a specific point-of-view that we respond to, whether it be positive or negative.

Art is never *one* definition.

Or, art is art.

When it comes to art, I always think of the best definition of "obscenity": We know it when we see it.

In that sense, then, one could say that art is the polar opposite of pornography.

6

Understanding art is a lifelong process.

When I was younger, I never cared much about art. Of course, I was greatly interested in the arts—movies, books, paintings. But art as a concept bigger than a group of paintings hung together in a museum did not begin to hit me until I turned 21 years old. Up until then, art as a way of life was vaguely defined, and as far as I was concerned, art meant museums filled with kids pointing and screaming, which usually left my eyes tired. Even now, museums still tire me after a few hours—the intensity of color, texture, and implied statements conveyed on the antiseptic walls leave my eyes begging for release from sensory overload.

7

The world out there is the biggest disability we will ever confront as artists.

We are not owed anything because the world is so narrow-minded. We artists are the harbinger of new ideas and attitudes to come. Time is our greatest ally when the world comprehends what we've already known for years, and our greatest enemy when we are confronted with the reality of our own mortality. When will we ever be recognized?

Being misunderstood by others who do not take the time to understand just what it is you're trying to create is a constant reality.

Patience and persistence combined with a little talent are probably the most essential virtues to have an artist of any stripe.

Art has nothing to do with how much hearing the artist has.

And art is not even a universal language. So much depends on our cultural upbringing that sometimes we do reject what is regarded as great artworks in other cultures.

When hearing people say that music is the universal language, they are lying.

I'd go further than that and say: Music is a universal lie.

Touch is the far more universal language. Touch is a far more honest and emotional truth than music could possibly ever hope to convey.

Our lives are determined not so much by whether we can comprehend the language of the majority culture, but by whether we feel loved which is conveyed over time through the touches we receive from each other. Studies have shown over and over again the inestimable power of touch upon children growing up; as easily surmised, the less-touched ones often turn violent from the inarticulation of not feeling as wanted.

9

If we don't want our deaf artists to stop inspiring the deaf community on to clearer expressions of themselves as an unique group, our insistence on labeling others within the deaf community has got to go.

"Nora's not deaf enough for us."

"Nick's not hearing enough for them."

"Why did Ned have to act so hard of hearing?" And so on.

When we start to deal with labels, we often get lost in the politics and lose sight of why we banded together in the first place: To communicate clearly without barriers. We start to overlook the truth of what the deaf artist is trying to share with us, and this nearsightedness easily kills more and more of our budding artists. Of course, that the backstabbing which often goes on in many marginalized communities different from our own is endemic to our community doesn't help.

10

If the baby boom of the 1940s and 1950s has taught us anything, it is that numbers have an undeniable influence on everything from politics to social mores to the arts. These babies, born after World War II, drove the American economy to unprecedented wealth; these babies, growing up, suddenly made the youth-oriented industries very, very rich, and gave voice and acted out a variety of concepts involving drugs, sex, censorship, activism, and so on. But most people haven't been aware of another kind of baby boom: Because of the rubella epidemic in the mid-1960s, we now have more deaf people living in America than at any other time in our history. Deaf people, wake up! This is *your* time.

What this means is an extraordinary opportunity to spark a genuine renaissance in the arts created by deaf people. Think about this again: More than at any other time in America have we had more deaf adults alive all at once.

11

For me, art *is* survival. The ecstasy of art inspires self-expression from within.

I share no interest in following anyone's theories but my own, nor do I expect anyone to follow my own. It is impossible to explicate directly how I create in the way I do; nothing can show directly my experience of the ecstasy itself. All art left behind is the aftermath of sheer ecstasy.

Art is the most dangerous path for a more meaningful truth, a place that reflects more deeply not only what it means to be deaf but more importantly, what it means to be human. Pretending to be a deaf artist and not looking at the human condition is cheating not only for yourself but also for the community you belong to; it makes you a hack artist whose work will not endure.

12

Does your work have to deal in some way with deafness? Heck, no!

Absolve yourself of responsibility to dogma and propaganda, and create in the name of truth and your obsessive themes.

13

Obsession is a terrific framework for exploring the infinite variations that is art.

For some artists, obsession is the nirvana of endless rediscovery.

In my work, I am obsessed with many things, but a common theme is sex. Not pornography per se, but the power of sex and sexual gratification in people's lives. The desire to be desired and to desire another is a wily force of nature.

14

Sometimes you've had a teacher or two say how good you are at painting, or drawing, or cooking, or whatever. Then you tried something a little more advanced, and your teacher would say, "Go with that, but do it with those two colors only."

Most deaf artists never have mentors who understand and encourage them to explore on their own, and to be the listening post for all their reports from the front. If a deaf high school student wants to become a professional actress, there are school plays to put on, but alternatives for learning on a high school level are scarce.

When I began to learn what it meant to be a writer, I desperately needed a mentor. I felt too different, and even I couldn't tell myself that what I was writing was indeed okay. For many years I wrote secretively and obsessively. To this day there remains a vast repository of work that will never see the light of day. They are simply my baby steps, full of awkwardness and mawkishness, toward a fuller articulation of the writer I would later become.

For the artist, the interaction between the art and the artists is essential to survival, yet the isolation of clear-eyed art from within is equally key to that survival.

15

Compassion is the initial impulse of creation. The word "compassion," according to *The American Heritage Dictionary of the English Language* (3rd Ed.), is a "deep awareness of the suffering of another coupled with the wish to relieve it." When a deaf person grows up in a hearing world, the deaf person wishes more than anything to make things easier not only for herself but for other deaf people after her. Many deaf people choose to go into the traditional professions of social services and education, mainly because they have not forgotten what it felt like to be shunted aside.

Others stick closely to home and their friends from the deaf residential schools, and endure dead-end jobs. Fewer still are encouraged to become artists, and so many of them feel afraid of expressing themselves creatively because they have seen others get backstabbed for trying.

To become an artist, a thick skin is mandatory. Even though the world seems to praise the artists who command huge sums in the marketplace, it has been exceptionally cruel to everyone else. If you don't have a thick skin, then perhaps you shouldn't try.

16

What qualifies as deaf art? To be honest with you, I don't even care. I am not in the least interested in those conferences in which the deafinition [*sic*] of art is being debated, because it's impossible to agree on such an issue. Sometimes I feel it is a waste of time.

This gives your creativity a fantastic leeway. It means that because no one agrees on anything, you might as well create whatever you want. It means that you can create *anything*. It means that you can be yourself as are. There are no boundaries inside you except yourself; away from the eyes of the world, you can create and reinvent yourself with your entire being.

17

"Interesting."

It is the one comment that all artists should never hope to be applied to their work.

"Interesting" is a very polite way of saying, "I don't get what you just did, but I don't want to hurt your feelings, so I'll say the next best thing."

It would be so much better if one said honestly, "I didn't get what you just did, so what were you trying to do here?"

When the artist tries to explain, she might discover accidentally why her intent hadn't been as clear as originally thought.

18

I like certain artists because their worldviews are so compelling and consistent. Long before I met him, I was completely enraptured by Quentin Crisp's writing. He was completely self-deprecating in his humor; later, the more I got to know him for nine years, the more I realized how completely unassuming he was. Once known as Denis Charles Pratt, he had managed to reinvent himself as Quentin Crisp in the 1920s when the world wasn't ready for an obvious poof who wouldn't change the way he dressed while walking about in London, and yet put forth this unforgettable persona that is no one else's but his alone; his wit is gently barbaric, yet incredibly compassionate. (His funny and completely engrossing autobiography *The Naked Civil Servant* remains a classic forty years after its publication.)

More than that, his life had become, for me, an enduring example of how one—even though Quentin would've thought that him being called an "artist" would be so preposterous, he was incredibly modest in spite of the attention showered on him—could stay true to one's own soul and find a rare enlightenment that wasn't merely spiritual, but also in all senses of being. Indeed, many of his quotes are classic examples of brevity, which can be found elsewhere in his writings.

His humble yet extraordinary life was art itself. He was beholden to no one but to the truth of his own philosophy of being. He was utterly himself unlike anyone I've ever met. It is not often that an artist could make her own life her art, but Quentin Crisp did.

19

I admire many great artists because they share one thing in common: They have reinvented themselves in their work and reinvent our *own* perspectives of the world in the process. Like them, I wish to reinvent myself. I no longer want to be that gawky underweight boy with a hearing aid harness hidden underneath his shirt. I no longer want to be that hormone-laden teenager falling in love with his own male classmates and teachers from afar. I no longer want to be that misfit who was seen as too smart by his deaf classmates in college. I no longer want to be that frustrated worker bee going to his dead-end job day in day out. I want to reinvent myself so that the real me can come out in the sunshine and play.

20

To reinvent yourself requires a certain kind of courage. I have had many dreams of wishing to have the ability to transform my body physically into someone else: I'd be a tiny woman in love with a Bunyanesque man, or I'd be a hustler trying to pick up a shy married businessman off Times Square, or I'd be a movie star ready for my sixteenth take under Martin Scorsese, or I'd be an aborigine coming across a discarded book that's in English. There are as many lives as there are dreams. I suspect, as James Thurber had, that we all have Walter Mitty in ourselves.

But alas, I am only human and my body can go only so far before collapsing. So I must reinvent myself every time I write. That's why I like to cross-pollinate across different genres in my writing and creativity. I want to pretend to be someone else, and I often do. When I am writing this, I imagine myself as a sixty-year-old college professor who's had had it with academia, and who's tired of all those handbooks that proclaim to teach you how to write, hardly taking into account that talent and fire, which cannot be bought at any price, are always the missing part of the equation to good writing—or art, for that matter.

21

1984 remains the most powerful novel I've ever read. It's taught me so much and has readied my sensibility for other works of art to come.

The first time I saw that book, my brother David kept saying, "How boring." I paid little attention because I, too, agreed that "Literature" was downright dry and boring.

A few years later, when I was in high school, we were required to read it. There was something alchemical about George Orwell's writing that I had to read the book twice—from beginning to end. Julia, Big Brother, Room 101—I still remember the creepy totalitarianism of the story. The description of Winston Smith being forced into Room 101 still spooks me to this day. Even though it's not a gay novel, one could interpret it as such: Winston's desire for love is strikingly parallel to a gay man's desire for love against all odds.

1984 is a heartbreaking story of love, but it's also about society trying to do away with the individualistic soul. As long as *1984* is read, there will always be people who evoke Big Brother warnings to remind us of our fading privacy in the face of technological advances that enable anyone to collect our most private date right beneath our noses. The book as a work of art is far more relevant today than when it was published in 1948. That remains the scary power of *1984*.

Art should take us out of ourselves and reimagine a new world if only to see how we could reimagine our own lives for the better.

22

I am thinking of everyone, perhaps, when I write, but I have a big confession to make.

I'm an extremely selfish person. When I write, I write for myself; I write what I'd like to read. I am my favorite reader, and my worst critic. Only in the process of creating can I forget the fact that I am deaf and whatever labels the world have assigned to me when I am out there among them; only that I am an artist in complete awe of his muse.

23

Before one can become an artist, there is a greater demon to deal with: Discipline.

My writing in the first ten years of my career is dreadful. I can't bear to read how awful I was back then; even now, I have a lot of reservations about whether I should keep or destroy these juvenile writings. But that's not the point: The only thing I've learned from writing in that first decade is discipline.

And how does one achieve some semblance of discipline?

Easy. Obsession.

Only through obsession with certain themes, concepts, images, sounds, and memories can we become enslaved to the joys of discipline.

24

What have I learned from being a deaf writer in the hearing world of publishing?

Editors don't care who you are. They do care whether you have anything to say. Most of these woefully underpaid folks have read hundreds and hundreds of letters and manuscripts from hopefuls to the point where they are able to detect that ringing, original, brilliant voice, often from the first page or two, from the clamorous pile of manuscripts shouting to be read. Sometimes editors are tired and overwhelmed, and they may miss as a result; but they're never too tired to know what makes them respond.

They scan your cover letters to see if you've done anything worth mentioning from a marketing perspective. The fact that you are a deaf writer means nothing—and everything—to them. This is especially true if you don't have a good agent attached.

Let me explain what I mean by "nothing." You shouldn't think that because you are deaf, you deserve red carpet treatment. For me, Gallaudet in 1984 was a revelation. All my life I had to deal with the sense of inequality of being deaf in a hearing world, and suddenly, when I learned ASL, I was equal to my peers. Gallaudet gave me a wonderful opportunity to accept myself as I am, so I could go back out there and not waste my tears over the sense of inequality that persisted in the hearing world.

Am I saying that we should swallow our pride and be meek in order to get what we really want— publication? Recognition? A huge pot of money?

Oh, no. No. Not at all.

One of the most important things I've learned from interacting with folks from publishing, theater, video, opera, journalism, film, dance, art, and other creative fields—and from having lived in New York for seventeen years—is this: Everyone wants to be famous. There's something in human nature that craves fame and recognition. Now, if every artist of every stripe wants to be famous, imagine the competition.

Hey—look at yourself. Not only do you want to earn some money, but you also want recognition for your hard work. Art is hard, I know. But you can't take rejection personally. You just have to keep trying.

Case in point: In May 1987, I took advantage of the Consortium program at Gallaudet and took a playwriting class at the Catholic University of America. It was there that I began writing my first serious play, *Snooty*. (I had written a few plays during my adolescence, but Snooty was my first as an adult.) In July 1990, *Snooty* won first place in the New York Deaf Theater's Sam Edwards Deaf Playwrights Competition, but nothing more came out of it until it was chosen by the National Theater of the Deaf (NTD) for a staged reading at their Deaf Theater Conference in July 1996. A director saw that staged reading and immediately wanted to get that play produced in Los Angeles. *Snooty* finally opened in May 1997—exactly ten years after I began writing the first draft. To be honest, if I'd known that it was going to take me that long, from Washington, D.C. to New York to Connecticut to California, I'd have thought long and hard about starting that play in the first place!

On the other hand, my play *Whispers of a Savage Sort* was picked up immediately by the First American Deaf Play Creators Festival only two months after I'd finished its second rewrite, and I had the most amazing folks involved—Howie Seago, who starred in the Oscar-nominated German sign language film *Beyond Silence*, was the director, and the cast had Phyllis Frelich, Nat Wilson, Patrick Graybill, Elena Blue, and Mel Westlake. They were just extraordinary. The play was later included in my collection of full-length plays *Whispers of a Savage Sort and Other Plays about the Deaf American Experience.*

Another example: I sent my play *Among Fathers* to NTD for workshop consideration for their next Deaf Theater Conference, but they turned it down. Instead of calling NTD a pile of epithets, I sent *Among Fathers* on to the Mark Taper Forum, easily the most prestigious theater in the Los Angeles area, that very same day. A month later they contacted me to say that my play was one of the five chosen out of dozens and dozens of submissions. Two months later I was flying out to Los Angeles to workshop *Among Fathers.*

It isn't just plays that took me a while to find homes for. *St. Michael's Fall* took me eight years to find a publisher; *This Way to the Acorns*, twelve years; *Men with Their Hands*, nineteen years; and *Mute*, twenty years. (Luckily, though, I don't seem to have to wait as long with my newer projects.)

So, when it comes to creating your work, you can't worry about how long it will take you to get it shown or published or produced. It's far more important to listen to your muse and to fine-tune whatever you want to say. The hours of listening will pay off, with a dab of luck, at the right time.

Luck is the accidental right timing that leads you to the opportunity to prove yourself. The best way to be prepared for Lady Luck when she calls is to keep working as if she will never ring the buzzer.

25

If you can understand that everyone—hearing or deaf, it doesn't matter—wants to be famous, it means that, unfortunately, being deaf isn't enough. It means that if you want to be taken seriously as an artist, you must have something to say that goes beyond labels—black, lesbian, grandfather, Korean, dog lover, Mexican, whatever—that will touch anyone who has a heart. When it comes to the human condition, labels are superficial. Always.

For example: I'm not Jewish, and I'm not an expert on the Holocaust. But *The Diary of Anne Frank* moved me because it wasn't just some Jewish girl writing about her life inside the Secret Annex for two years but because it was about being an outcast living with a family of outcasts in a world that didn't want them there. You can replace the label "Jewish" with the word "deaf" and the story wouldn't change at all. She could've been writing about the deaf community in the years when oralism was primarily taught everywhere. Anne Frank said in so many words: We are a people who deserve to survive because we are just like you—human and vulnerable. We suffer just like you. And the remarkable thing was, she wasn't trying to speak for the Jewish people, only for herself: Humanity, please. *Humanity.* That's why people still respond to her work today some sixty years after her death.

That's what I aim for in my own work. It's not enough to indicate that some girl is deaf, some boy is hard of hearing, and his mother is hearing. It doesn't mean anything to people who don't know deaf culture. But if you say the girl feels shy because she has a severe acne problem, that gets to us much more quickly than learning that she is deaf. Why? We all have felt at one time or another insecure about our appearances. Same thing with the boy: He is constantly dreaming of designing spaceships, even in class. Not everyone might connect with designing better rockets, but everyone will connect to that feeling of boredom in class. And what about the mother? She has to restrain her own temper because she can't shake her hatred for her menial salesclerk job at K-mart. We can certainly relate to that feeling of wanting to blow up because the world feels so stupid. Why do I have to do this lousy job when I deserve better? And so on. Thus, labels are superficial; feelings are not.

So, if deaf artists want to be taken seriously, they have to look beyond labels and look deeper into the human condition. Why are we here? Why do we have to suffer? Why do we love? And all the big tasty questions that are so impossible to answer yet give artists countless opportunities and angles to explore what it means to be human in spite of our impossibly short and frail lifetimes.

26

Most hearing people don't care about deafness. They might be fascinated with the idea of sign language, but the subtext is "novelty." As you already know, deaf people are not a novelty with a cute language. We are a *real* people. So how can we move forward if no one takes us seriously?

Surprise, surprise: You have inside of you the best gift any artist can ever ask for. What's that? You have the gift of outsiderhood.

Think about the great works of literature, and what many of them have in common. Just one thing, really. All the compelling heroes and villains share with us the feeling of being an outsider, of differentness, even if they are accepted by the society they live in; in spite of their circumstances, they want acceptance on a deeper level. This craving is absolutely universal. But the point of view varies profoundly, as do our life experiences.

And unique points of view are what editors and other powers-that-be are often looking for. You know firsthand what it feels like to be different. Every art seeker wants to spend time with those who can articulate and share their feelings of being different.

27

If we deaf artists choose not to depict the deaf experience in a variety of ways in our work, we must try to tackle the enormous responsibility of exploring the human condition.

We shouldn't require each other to write about deafness all the time. After all, we know a lot more than that. But we should expect each other to look deeper into the human condition.

A human life may be short, but human nature is forever.

The proliferation of mobile reading devices such as the iPad and the Kindle has made the ebook revolution a viable reality. The frustrations many writers had experienced with the rules of legacy publishing (e.g., paper) evaporated with the possibility of self-publishing ebooks. Compared to the time-consuming process of submitting a book for an editor's consideration, negotiating the contract, going back and forth on the edits, laying out the book, poring over the galleys, working with the cover designer, and having the book finally printed, readying the manuscript for a variety of ebook formats and uploading the book soon after is a snap, and shockingly so. It's also nice that most ebook publishers offer an unusually hefty royalty, usually in the range of 50% to 70% of the retail price. It's high time that writers earn more for their hard labors.

I've downloaded a vast number of self-published ebook samples, usually the first chapter or two, on my iPad. Quality varies wildly, naturally, but most glaring is the fact that a vast majority amply demonstrates in the first few pages the reason why they weren't accepted by publishers in the first place. They stink. I can forgive their choice of lame cover designs, but what's unforgivable is sloppy writing. Some of them are poorly edited, if at all, right down to the incorrect usage of punctuation and spelling typos. It's always a shock to find misspellings on the first page! A lot do not have a compelling "voice," or a sense of rhythm that would make me sit up and take notice. (See the first few pages of any of these novels to see what I'm talking about: *The Handmaid's Tale*, Margaret Atwood;

The Beans of Egypt, Maine, Carolyn Chute; *You Must Remember This*, Joyce Carol Oates; *The Passion*, Jeanette Winterson; and so on. Such stories grab your attention and they never let go. How thrilling it is to be warmed by the fireplaces of their imaginations! It's pretty hard to top a well-written story wrought with great care.)

Just because the self-publishing ebook revolution has made it possible for novice writers to get "published" instantly doesn't mean that we readers should lower our expectations and standards. And what's more, the more self-published books stink, the more readers will return to publishers who do take the time to screen out bad writing and bring out books by good writers. If that's the case, the ebook revolution will only prove to have been a spectacular exercise in shoddy writing. That some major New York publishers are getting into the business of self-publishing by setting up separate branches worries me. Vanity and greed make the most peculiar and persistent bedfellows.

There's a silver lining to the ebook phenomenon, however. For some writers, their out-of-print titles from legacy publishers are finding second lives as ebooks. Those are great, because they've already been edited the first time around. And I advise those who still wish to self-publish: Hire the toughest editor you can find, and be willing to listen. Not everything you write is great. The secret to good writing is tough yet constructive editing before it goes out in the world. Talent alone isn't enough; an editor's objectivity is a crucial part of the bargain.

I would imagine that in time, self-publishing won't leave the same stain on one's literary reputation as was the way in the past, but as long as writers are willing to work with experienced editors, the ebook revolution may prove not to be such a bad thing.

Whenever you enter a contest or submit your work to an editor, rejection should never be taken as a sign of failure. It simply means that you must continue to read, read, and *read*, and write. Do *not* give up. Real artists never do.

That's the most important thing I've learned from writing my play *Snooty* in the first place, and that took me ten years to learn. (I'm still learning this with my other projects!)

Once an artist understands rejection can she begin to embrace the exhilarating freedom of expressing without boundaries between strangers.

30

The best way to deal with rejection is to forget about it *before* it happens.

I send my work out to the powers-that-be and *forget about it.* This is very important. If I obsess over whether I'll get accepted, I'll feel entirely too crushed when I get the rejection notice. But the funny thing is, if I force myself to forget it—not always easy, I know—I don't feel disappointed when I get rejected. I'm already on to the next thing.

Better yet is the gift of forgetfulness when I get a completely unexpected notice of acceptance. Such a pleasant blessing can last for days.

31

I am often asked this question: "Why do you write?" My answer, which I hope will be yours too, is: "Why do you breathe?"

Art is like breathing, except that when you breathe it in, your body undergoes a transformation, however slight it may be. Somehow, for a fleeting second, something has changed in the way you perceive the world, and you may find yourself dealing with its repercussions for the rest of your life.

Sometimes a work of art can be so great that your feelings about it can evolve over time. One of my favorite paintings is Andrew Wyeth's *Christina's World* (1948). A young woman whose face we never see is stranded on the autumnal grasses of a wide field, her body contorted, as she reaches out to the stark house in the far distance.

I was in my early teens when I first saw that painting in an art book. My reaction was "Interesting."

When I became more aware of the disability rights movement by the late 1980s, the painting took on a whole other meaning. It was almost as if Wyeth was telling us: "Look how helpless this crippled girl is!"

When I saw the actual painting at the Museum of Modern Art, I reacted differently. The mysterious Christina seemed to be defiant, expecting the relentlessly brutal world to accept her as she was. And the painting techniques that Wyeth used to convey such a multi-layered image of enormous feeling and compassion were nothing short of extraordinary. And the painting was physically smaller than I thought it would be!

This bears repeating in light of *Christina's World*: Art is a specific point of view that we respond to, whether it be positive or negative.

When I talk about the word, I refer to the much more volatile bible of human nature. Like much of William Shakespeare's work, the bible of human nature is a collective work that is constantly revised, updated, abridged, and distorted beyond recognition. Art reflects that very nature itself, which is why for some people art so easily offends. Even when the work of art seems orderly, it somehow insists on the very messiness of life itself. The nature of art should be subversive, if only because of how we tend to think and yet not share. In the face of society itself, the fact that we have free thoughts at all is the very heart of subversion!

Anarchy of the mind is a beautiful thing, and even greater is the resulting shotgun marriage of beauty and chaos that endures in art.

Artists risk ridicule and scorn just to reflect the mirror back on their enemies, who feel insulted. The irony is that while the artist may play with certain elements to highlight a truth, she does not exaggerate. Society lies because truth hurts too much. Art tells the truth, and the artist often suffers when society is not willing to listen. Once in a while, fame and fortune is the unexpected windfall, but if the artist has truly endured for her craft's sake, she will know that adulation and wealth aren't everything.

33

I'm always amused when I hear about this or that deaf activist wishing to keep ASL "pure," especially when ASL was originally adapted from French Sign Language (through our first deaf American teacher, Laurent Clerc, no less!) and combined with signs used by the local deaf community in Hartford, Connecticut; doesn't that sound like what happened to English? Likewise, art should never be pure. It should never claim to be. The more bastardized and polluted it is, the more it will touch more of us in the most unexpected ways. Art is give-and-take. We should avoid pretentiousness and elitism at all costs. Brevity, accessibility, and poetry are qualities sorely lacking among those who claim to be artists. If you are brief and clear, your poetry—whether on screen, canvas, or page—can turn into succinct magic.

34

Our power to communicate much more clearly to get what we truly want is magnified if we study poetry. Some poems, I agree, simply suck and should not be taught in schools. In fact, I think the best way to teach poetry in high school is to discuss why poetry sucks. That would get their attention, and by getting their attention, they can begin to look at how poetry can be so cool.

We live in a culture in which movies and sports rule. Books are an afterthought; the general state of this country's educational system frustrates me more than anything else. How could students possibly master the full potential of language—whether ASL or English or any other language—if they do not begin to comprehend the power of poetry?

At its best, poetry is pitch-perfect condensation. In a poem, a word alone isn't a word alone. It is a building block, a signpost to something greater than the sum of its parts. A word chosen is chosen for a specific reason; if a few, all the better.

Poetry demands a microscope. If you know how the molecular structure of each word contributes to the overall DNA of that poem, you've unlocked the key to clearer communication, and therefore power.

35

Words are intangible. They are symbols for what cannot be truly encompassed; I can only pray that others can decode the full meaning of what I wish to share. Words can be tangible, but only on paper. Otherwise, we continue to store terabytes of words in our memory banks; if our brains were dissected, there would remain nothing so much as a word to be found. Regardless of the discipline in which the artist chooses to convey her vision, other elements—color, smell, sound, shape, and so on—can have an equally intangible and tangible weight. The clash—and the harmony—of all these elements can produce unforgettable sensations that linger long after we've forgotten why we came to experience that particular work in the first place.

However imperfect its means may be, art is the best method we have of passing human understanding and wisdom from one generation to the next, and beyond.

Human nature has changed very little since the beginning of time; it is another thing to discover the fact that old men and women were not always wise, or that the need for connecting with one another has remained the same. Experiencing the old works give us the particular pleasure of knowing that my generation was not alone with our problems, although ours are much more intrinsically linked to the larger—and global—village of how we live and where we are headed.

37

Language, and its representation in a variety of artistic forms, is an ever-changing constant. It is a static flux in which both little and enormous dramas of our lives revolve: misunderstanding, prejudice, and the fear of being known for what we really are. This fear of the latter—and the desire to expose it—is palpable in many great works of art. As a result, artists are far more emotionally naked and yet they often risk all to share with us what they've experienced.

38

I remember trying to write in tiny perfect letters in a diary so I could save up more space for all the things I had to say. More than three decades later I find that while I have many things I'd like to say, I'm more concerned with saying them well instead of saying them all. When I reached that point, I was no longer a wanna-bee buzzing for fame and fortune. Because I had learned that writing doesn't always pay well, I felt I had nothing much to lose by gravitating toward the richness of art.

Emotional honesty is crucial to your art. If you lie to yourself in your own creative processes, everyone will detect that false note much more quickly than you're willing to admit. If you force your own work to accommodate a prefabricated political agenda because you feel obligated to do so, you are a liar.

And no one likes liars.

You are not looking at the experience from within; you are looking at the experience from the outside. You are not thinking in terms of being human; you are thinking in terms of being right and wrong, which is politics.

At the end of my play *Whispers of a Savage Sort*, which explores backstabbing within a small town deaf community, the audiences learn that the bowling money, which precipitated the backstabbing throughout the play, was merely misplaced. Many people have told me that they didn't like this non-committal ending, but I still stand by that ending. *Who* took the money was not the point; *how* others reacted to the situation, and began to destroy each other because of politics, was much more interesting. That by itself was a much more potent statement than I could've made had I chosen to blame So-and-So for the disappearance of the bowling membership fees, or shown the audience who took the money early on in the story.

This is why I rail so often against political correctness. Life is never politically correct, so why should art?

40

The word in its own way comforts me with the knowledge that I am no different from anyone else. The written word for me is a fulcrum between two worlds: Mine is interior, and theirs flaunted and printed for all to see. The hearing and the deaf do not know what my world is like. This is not because I am deaf but because like all artists, I place a peculiar faith in all the elements of my craft. I can only suggest; artists possess the power of mere suggestion. The tension between such intangibles—ideas, sounds, colors—and tangibles—book, canvas, CD—pervades all art. This is why those who believe in the redemption of art can never really claim to know anyone else but herself.

Art by itself is boring and static; it is our responses that make art come alive in selfish ways. Art becomes about *our* own reactions and experiences.

41

As my love and respect for the written word continues well into my fourth decade, I find myself becoming much more assertive. I no longer worry whether certain topics will offend; instead I am more concerned with the pulse, and the craft, of my writing. At one time, I had tried to use a pseudonym for my gay short stories, but now I refuse to hide beyond it. Was I that ashamed of the content of my own work, or did I want to be known as I am, not as someone else?

I hope to be understood and recognized, and if such a thing is possible, to be loved for what I do.

42

In a final analysis, art is redemption. It forces us to confront the ugly parts of ourselves in order to celebrate the beautiful parts of ourselves. If we do not experience rain, we can never appreciate the sunshine that come our way. The artist accepts both good and bad, both light and dark, both quietness and loudness. Life is simply there to be experienced from A to Z, and beyond numbers and infinity. Not being afraid to experience life as it is, by itself, is redemption that all artists at heart experience.

True artists are not selfish with their creative impulses; they wish to share with us what they have learned so that we, too, could learn to embrace life as it is instead of constantly bemoaning how horrible life is and wishing why do our lives have to be so miserable. Life is. Art is. They reflect each other. They cannot be severed, for to shatter either mirror is to shatter our own chances of redemption.

43

In the same way for many deaf people, to give up ASL is to give up their own sense of belonging. Our hands are our anchors, and many of us choose to stay in the same harbor because we know what's expected of us in all that's familiar all around us. The deaf artist often feels homesick for her people not because she's away from them—in fact, she probably mingles constantly among them—but because there aren't enough deaf people who understand what being an artist means in the first place. Like most hearing people who don't have much of a clue to what being an artist means (beyond the kind starving and making bare-bones money just outside their peripheral vision and the somehow-well-off kind depicted in movies), many deaf people may think that artists make a lot of money. After all, some Japanese guy paid *millions* for just one Vincent Van Gogh painting. And that Hollywood screenwriter Joe Eszterhas made a ton of money off his scripts such as *Basic Instinct* and *Showgirls*, but where is he now? (*Showgirls* is a spectacular example of bad writing veering unintentionally into camp.) In highlighting such arbitrary exceptions, the media implies that artists are often overpaid. Not true.

Because marketed hype is often motivated by someone's desire to make money, it doesn't necessarily mean the hyped artist is making a worthy comment. A living, perhaps, but art? In order to make her art palatable to the broadest audience possible, the artist must constantly compromise down to the common denominator of whatever feels safe and familiar. This is particularly true of films, because they cost so much to make in the first place; many great filmmakers manage to straddle the line between art and commerce. Even then, I believe filmmaking is an art into itself, which explains why I'm always annoyed whenever people have to talk to me while we are both watching the same picture. Behind each image flickering on the screen are hundreds of people who have toiled hours and days just to execute and perfect that fleeting second; I want to show them respect in the same way I hope my viewers and readers would show me respect by seeing and reading my work to see what I have to say.

Artists have a great responsibility to pay attention to their colleagues, for they too feel underappreciated. Just listening alone—or the lack of it—often makes or breaks the artist's spirit. I know it has made a difference in mine.

45

Art is insidiously pervasive when it comes to influencing the masses' view of deafness. Awareness may help, but art does influence writers—hearing or deaf—in giving *their* own version of deafness, which in turn influences future writers' attitudes toward deafness. This is why deaf-accurate input on projects involving deafness and deaf characterizations is so paramount to the believability factor of such elements.

Because I had been so concerned with how deaf people were characterized in Hollywood films, I once wrote an open letter to the actor Sean Penn.

Dear Mr. Penn:

I am sure that your agent is constantly deluged with a ton of screenplays, so I am not going to try pitching any of my scripts here. Aside from your incredible body of work as an actor and director, you seem to be a man of integrity, always wanting to do the right thing whether in art or politics. Please think about these few considerations should you find committed financing behind a script featuring a signing deaf character.

Is the deaf character three-dimensional? We don't need any more stories in which deaf characters are reduced to the weighty symbolism of how poetic their hands are, or how more "powerful" their silence is. That's an immediate tip-off that the script was probably written by hearing people who watched older films featuring deaf characters as part of their "research." In turn, these older films were written by hearing people who probably did very little homework about the deaf community! Anyone who's spent a substantial amount of time among the deaf signing community will realize that we are just people who don't see ourselves as disabled. (Try visiting a deaf signing party without an interpreter. Feel lost already? Now you're disabled. Not us.) Ignorance about our information accessibility needs is far more of a disability than our defective ears. As with any traits that make any character unique and distinctive, deafness alone isn't enough. It's actually boring. And please say no to scripts that rehash the clichés of music versus muteness, speech versus sign, or cochlear implants. More than anything else, please ask to work with a deaf scriptwriter instead of just working with an American Sign Language (ASL) consultant. (Yes, Mr. Penn, I am naturally available.)

Is the character written to be "inspiring" in a realistic way? Not every gay person is inspiring, but Harvey Milk was. Mr. Milk wasn't a hottie. He wasn't rich either. He was an ordinary man who tried to master the intricacies of politics. In doing so, however, he actually galvanized the gay rights movement and made "coming out" a requirement in order to wake up the rest of the country to realize that they, too, were just ordinary people like them and make it harder for straight people to think of gay people as child molesters. (Never mind the fact that there are far more straight molesters simply because there are more straight people out there, period. If one goes by such numbers alone, straight people should not be allowed to teach children.) Wouldn't it be nice to have hearing people wake up and realize that us deaf people are ordinary as they are? Just because we can't hear as well as they shouldn't have to make us "inspirational." Many able-bodied people still believe that our "disabilities" are something to be overcome when in reality their patronizing attitudes toward us have proven far more disabling than whatever disability we may have. I caught a sense of that in your totally credible performance as a mentally-disabled father in the film *I Am Sam*.

Just how much signed dialogue is the deaf character expected to do? If it's a lot, I dare you to master ASL and not have your dialogue cropped by the camera's frame, and have a few deaf people watch the footage and see how well you pass as a Deaf person. (You don't know why that word was capitalized? A small detail like that is something of a litmus test for us Deaf people to see whether you've actually done your homework. The uppercase "D" refers to Deaf people who see themselves culturally deaf and use sign language to communicate; the lowercase "d" refers to deaf people who can speak well enough not to feel the need for signing.) Many deaf people hate it when the cinematographer captures all of a Deaf person's signing but masks most of a hearing person's clumsy signs. It's almost insulting. Mimicking signs isn't the same as mimicking dialogue from another language phonetically; it's way much harder, and you can't go into the studio to fix a flubbed word. What you see is what you're stuck with. That's why I dare you to try out ASL first and see how it feels on your hands.

Finally, does the Deaf character have friends? This may seem strange, but having a Deaf character with no friends continues to perpetuate the myth of social isolation that goes with being unable to speak well. Yes, that may seem dramatic in terms of angst but it is becoming more offensive. I believe you can still have heightened drama among signing friends. While I am unable to judge the accuracy of Japanese Sign Language used by the hearing actress Rinko Kikuchi playing a Deaf character in Alejandro Gonzalez Inarritu's film *Babel*, I was thrilled to see that she had a number of Deaf friends.

In my involvement with the Deaf community since 1984, I've met four or five hearing people who signed so fluently that I actually thought they were Deaf at first! (With one exception being a talented interpreter, they were all "children of Deaf adults," or CODAs.) The tell-tale signs of "hearingness" are subtle, but they are definitely there and easy to catch with our Deaf eyes. It's really difficult to pass as a Deaf person, Mr. Penn, because we've had to sharpen our eyes as a matter of survival.

I would suggest that if you really like the script, please sign on as an executive producer or even as director, and cast a Deaf person in the part. That actor will bring an authenticity and depth of experience to the part that a hearing non-signer cannot fake. We do not walk the streets in fear because we cannot hear what transpires in shadow. We do not ache to hear music the same way you do; many of us enjoy it in our own ways. We do not feel helpless with our lack of speech; we've already figured out how to communicate with people who feel helpless with their lack of sign. Like Gus Van Sant has shown so well with the gay community in the film *Milk*, we too are a proud people with issues. We are human, and thankfully so. Our humanity is what keeps the language of hands breathing long after we're dead.

Mr. Penn, I appreciate your time and consideration. Should you like to discuss more, please have your people call my people.

Sincerely,
Raymond Luczak

Art is projection of the realness from the artist's soul. We react strongly as a result.

Without experiencing art in a real and passionate way, our lives begin to absorb the usual gray-colored grind—basketball and other sports tournaments, bills to pay, gossip, our children, the news that seem to overlap online, the latest sexual conquest.

Our souls will in no time feel gray, and we fall into a slumber worse than death: A wearying time of wondering how to articulate those murky feelings lurking inside of ourselves, and giving up on the very notion of communicating ourselves *as we are*, which is what art tries to do.

Art is communication at its very best.

48

Art isn't necessarily about how much college education you've acquired.

Art demands from us an openness to new ideas and experiences, for it is already open and inviting us in.

In fact, snobbery is an evil trait. Low-brow culture can have as much to offer as high-culture.

Persistence is the mask of the artist. She creates for herself, whether she has the money or not. She is often too busy listening to her own muse and yet listening beyond her eyes to the world around them. But before she can listen to her muse well, she must know the history and rules of her chosen field first. Once she understands on a pure gut level *why* many of those restrictive rules were created and put into place, she will make a marvelous rule-breaker and make her own voice sing differently from anyone else's.

With such rules broken, the artist must listen with her entire body to the muse and the world in stereo. She must create herself and her identity as an artist in stereo.

Hacks create in mono. There are hardly any surprises. Hacks thrive on clichés and the perceived stupidity of their audiences.

Having first the foundation of tradition in place is the essential recipe for the confidence needed to break rules and rediscover what it means to be an artist on her own terms and rise above hacks who fear too much sweat and originality.

50

Art as a concept has gotten an understandably bad rap in recent years as in "Oh, that painting with nothing but white on a square is called 'art'? And sold for $60,000? Why, any idiot could paint that!" Moreover, with that kind of thinking, we have more hacks thinking they can make a cool sixty grand too. The Oscar-nominated documentary *Exit through the Gift Shop: A Banksy Film* is riveting and ultimately depressing. Obsessed with street art and pop culture, a man decides that he's an artist, proceeds to spend a fortune on his first show, and makes a ton of money thanks to the hype.

So many deaf artists claim to be such that I hesitate in deciding just *whom* the true artists of the bunch are. I prefer to absorb everything because both persistence and discipline might make the work of an amateur a revelation. You never know.

51

No one wants to say it, but deaf theater is considered "exotic."

It's not performed enough, and not enough people go. Perhaps that's always been the story of theater considered too "different" from the rest of society. The irony is that many of the experiments that are attempted today in those way-out-of-the-way places become standards in tomorrow's mainstream theater. Alternative theater is not about predicting the future of theater, but it does pump a lot of inspiration into the lifeblood of theater itself; the playwright must experiment freely if tomorrow's audiences demand to be entertained in new and exciting ways.

52

Going to a good show put on by a deaf theater company gives me pleasure for many reasons. But I confess to enjoying bad shows and films sometimes because they continue to teach and remind me what elements of storytelling doesn't work, and *why*. For me as a deaf playwright and filmmaker, it's an ongoing lesson.

53

Just as technological advances have made many deaf people's lives easier, it means that more hacks will never experience the *true* discipline and understanding of tradition and the rules in their craft, which in turn gives us more garbage, which in turn adds to the bad rap that art has been getting lately. It doesn't help that hacks has always outnumbered artists or that major talent can be so hard to find amidst their white-noise din. No wonder why a critical appreciation of a true artist's work strikes me as a miracle.

54

In an email discussion among deaf writers that I'm on, one writer made a compelling observation about hearing critics. (Her comments have been edited for clarity.)

During the DeafWay II conference in Washington, D.C., local art critics refused to review the work of the international deaf artists on exhibit. They said they couldn't; that it would be like "telling someone in a wheelchair how to walk."

Some time later, I learned about a group of deaf American artists meeting to discuss various art-related questions. One of the attendees said, essentially, that "We don't have to wait for hearing critics to review us. We can write our own reviews."

Which is true, we can. But I also thought that hearing critics not reviewing deaf artists means—or could mean—that their various courses of study had not prepared them to write about *everyone*. And if we underwrite their silence by "doing our own reviews," their *silence* will be perpetuated.

55

A friend told me what she thought was a funny story about two deaf teenage girls who roomed together at a residential school for the deaf. They were seniors, and they had their own computers at opposite ends of the room. There wasn't a wall between them. Somehow or other they fell into an argument. They had their backs to one another, but they weren't any more than ten feet apart. Through their instant-messaging program, they were typing angrily at each other.

She laughed and laughed.

I stood there, horrified. How are these two girls going to communicate with their own future spouses when they have an argument?

The more high-tech we become, the more we will require high-touch. If we don't get enough of the touch we need in order to feel affirmed as human beings, we will become emotional train wrecks, trying so hard to find the rails that once held us steady and true.

It isn't love only that must save us. Art too.

56

The problem with the popularity of social media such as Facebook and Twitter is that we are losing sight of each other as *people*, as flesh and bones. We've reduced ourselves to status updates and tweets. You might think that's not true, but how else can you explain the reality of how few people show up at deaf events? We've become too busy for each other.

Have we become so jaded that we feel we don't need to see each other in person? Will future generations stumble in the fading art of communicating in person and feel emotionally safer behind an Internet-connected device? What will be the new definition of "community"?

Perhaps art from the past and the present will have much more to teach the future.

57

On one of my bookshelves is a framed postcard that I picked up in an art museum during one of my trips to Chicago. White letters proclaim on a black background: FEAR NO ART. It was one of those things I bought on a whim, but as time went on, the saying has resonated with me more and more. Upon reflection, those three words say so much—almost too much, actually!

It isn't just about censorship. It means that if we don't have art, we're no longer human. We might as well be animals. Historically, until about two hundred years ago, most deaf people weren't educated because many hearing people held the mistaken view that if one couldn't speak, one couldn't be taught. It is no accident that many hearing writers of yore saw us deaf people who signed as "barbarians." Sometimes the word "savages" was used to describe us as if our lack of legible speech demanded our redemption on their own terms, which of course was a predisposition for automatic failure.

The more I think about it, the more I realize how badly we deaf artists need a new postcard. This time it should say: FEAR NO SIGNS.

For writers who aim to become artists, the computer can be a curse in disguise. Editors say that because it's now so easy to write/revise/edit on the computer, the amount of submissions continues to increase each year. I can't imagine how more slipshod the printed word will be like once voice-recognition software becomes more accurate in transcribing. Deaf writers, having to think a little bit about the words they write because they have to type themselves, do have a clear advantage in this regard. Likewise, the artist must battle the temptation of easy replication to stay honest and true to her own craft.

The artist's talent, presentation, and determination are enough. But of course, a little luck can go a long way.

Luck is a very peculiar thing. Who knows why some of us are blessed with more of it than others, and why some who are clearly more talented than the lucky ones are forced to await their turn, which may never come?

A few years ago I read *Outliers: The Story of Success*, a book by Malcolm Gladwell. He believed that there was a unifying connection among a divergence of people who succeeded at the top of their fields. It didn't matter what field—sports, business, entertainment, or technology—they excelled in. What mattered was the fact that each of these individuals had practiced and worked hard for at least 10,000 hours before they started to get noticed. Gladwell calculated the hours of practice and work invested by various leaders and artistic successes to see if this observation was true. Some of those "outliers," he felt, weren't always spectacularly talented, but the fact that they'd kept at it for so long, usually in a supportive environment, eventually rewarded them.

Of course, it isn't as simple as all that. Fortuitous timing—otherwise known as the proverbial "big break"—plays a huge factor here. Still, these people had been practicing for so long that when they were given opportunities, they were primed enough to spin them into even more opportunities.

I'm not sure if Gladwell's theory of "outliers" is solid, but it does make for provocative reading. Anything that jolts us into viewing the world a little differently is always a good thing.

61

One of my favorite artists to grace the walls and the shelves of my apartment is André Pellerin.

When he creates his ceramics on the spinning wheel, the contours and textures made evident by the instinctual movements of his powerful fingers and tools become a language that is impossible to translate. His choice of colors and glazes becomes layers that add to the complexity of the seeming non-drama that is a simple bowl. My responses don't come from the fact that I've known him for so many years; it's the reality of how insistently tactile the craft of pottery is. He has failed so many times, usually for reasons beyond his control—the kiln wasn't hot enough, the air was too humid, and so on—but that's never stopped him. Each potter has her own style, and through that style is a signature that says: *This is me*—right now—*at the time*.

I've enjoyed watching Pellerin's work evolve over the years from simple vases and plant pots in earth colors into elaborate and bigger pieces laced with color. He isn't afraid to try incorporating other elements, such as dirt dug from the ground or reeds, in his pots. When he isn't working on his ceramics, he has painted paper flowers that he'd cut out in a variety of colors and created 3-D bouquets of them to be hung in shadowboxes. He has created seasonal mosaics out of tiles. And just now he's told me he's exploring making paper sculptures. I was blown away when he showed me on the videophone his first few attempts at paper sculptures. A single piece of paper and a series of well-placed razor cuts for folds could create a 3-D staircase without glue? I had no idea!

Some might feel agog at the idea of a deafblind artist who is totally visual, but as he has enough vision to do what he loves doing, I don't sit in amazement at the notion like a hearing person in awe of Helen Keller might be. Just like living as a deaf person is not any better or worse than living as a hearing person, so it is with being a deafblind person.

In order to discover new things amidst the occasional tiredness of our art, we need to screw up. Shake it all up. Start all over again. Impose new limitations on ourselves when we try to create something new.

Making mistakes is absolutely wonderful. As a writer, I never tell anyone anything about the first draft of whatever I'm working on because I want to give myself full permission to fail. You read that right: I need to fail. I want to score a huge flopperoo in the safety net of my own computer with no one looking over my shoulder. No one has to know how terrible my initial attempts at a new poem were—or anything for that matter.

The most important thing is to get it all out. Do not judge yourself while you create. Do not think about what others might think. Do not censor yourself. But most of all, do not lie to yourself.

No matter how rough-hewn, unassailable truth in art can be stunning and unforgettable. Even an accidental brushstroke of the wrong color on an otherwise perfectly composed painting can be beautiful even as it is jarring. We will remember that single brushstroke far longer than the painting itself. I don't see that as a bad thing. It is merely a reflection of how we are constantly forgetting to look at the bigger picture of whatever we're experiencing.

So please: Fail. *Fail*. Fail!

When you fail so much and you don't give up, you'll find yourself succeeding in ways you didn't expect. Accidents can be so revelatory and beautiful.

Brilliant failures fascinate me a lot more than soulless masterpieces.

Growing up, I was aware of Barbra Streisand, but I never cottoned to her like many of my hearing friends. I could tell that from her appearances on television, she had a good voice, but that was it. I liked a few cuts from *Guilty*, her biggest-selling album, but that was all I liked of her work.

Then my ex-partner in New York, who was a huge Streisand fan, brought home her four-CD box set *Just for the Record . . .*, a retrospective of mostly unreleased material. In it were eight live cuts recorded in 1962 at the Bon Soir Club that would've been a part of her debut album. Those songs were a revelation—she wasn't fastidious at all. She sang full-throttle with shrieks while still hitting high notes. *This was Barbra Streisand?!?* Whatever happened to that girl who hadn't cared about orchestrated gloss, but raw with genuine emotion? We don't need any more music that's so overproduced—or so Auto-Tuned—that it emits only faint squeaks of emotion.

Give me a brilliant failure anytime.

64

Even though I am gay, I've always thought of my muse as exquisitely female. I see her very much as a temptress with a bowl of green grapes. Once she offers me a grape of something new, I can't stop eating. I must finish the bowl. When the bowl is empty, I have a first draft. Rewriting becomes dessert.

When I am not inspired, everything becomes a fattening snack filled with empty calories. Yet I've learned not to be too worried; not all snacks are bad. I just needed some fuel for the backburner of my imagination before my next, and often *very* orgiastic and very unexpected, feast.

Creating is a cycle that never ends. Up, down, and far too many aimless long rides on a paved road cutting through the desert. You think your own life is the same old thing, but your craft is not the same old thing. Your art is sustaining you in ways that mere shelter, food, and sex can't. You are *not* a perfunctory human being with a hearing problem. You have experienced solutions that aren't even solutions to the untrained eye, and live with the questions that constantly energizes you to create.

Art is about problem-solving. Why did Anna Karenina fling herself in front of that train? In Leo Tolstoy's eyes, we experience the breadth of Russian society in her life, and living with Anna, we come to the same conclusion as she did: Society is a bitch. Tolstoy doesn't offer us solutions because he already knew that each person has many solutions within herself. He observes, and reshapes his observations, to allow us to reobserve the familiar with unfamiliar eyes.

So do all the great artists since the beginning of recorded time.

67

The artist always masters the language of her chosen craft before she bends and breaks the rules to accommodate her unique vision. This explains partly why poetry has gotten such a bad name—*too* many poets seem to think that arbitrary line breaks within a sentence constitutes a poem. No, no—the properties of each word and all its possible connotations/denotations should be weighed by itself and finally with all the rest to see if the poem can achieve a specific, and unforgettable, response. Recently I came across Timothy Murphy's poem "The Quarrel." Its simplicity absolutely blew me away.

> Climbing in sullen silence past treeline
> where blasted spruces drunkenly incline,
> we stumble on two racks of caribou.
> Clasped in a deadlock neither bull could break
> they bleach beside a frigid Yukon lake—
> amateurs who never locked horns with you.

That is the power of compression inherent in poetry itself. Likewise, art should be so compressed that when we begin to decompress a great work, it should overwhelm us with its reach and power. Art is a matter of stripping away to show us what really matters, and the rest will take care of itself.

Art is a dry sponge waiting for our perceptions to water it into its fullness.

Art should reward us for trying.

Art should give us more than the physical object itself. We should come away with the experience of sensation that never leave us, so much that we feel compelled to revisit the work immediately, or again over the years. Movies are a great example.

I own a copy of Peter Jackson's *Heavenly Creatures* on Blu-Ray, but seeing that movie (subtitled, of course), I get the inestimable joy of seeing how well the various elements of suspense, fantasy, eroticism, and death-wish are fused together in the disjointed process of filmmaking to create an unified work of art, a revelation that still enthralls. The home video formats may change over the years, but the images and performances in *Heavenly Creatures* will still linger in my mind.

The scarcity of artists within the deaf community is made more difficult because we don't seem to want to recognize each other. In a way, we are deathly afraid of being backstabbed by our own colleagues and being overshadowed by what we perceive as their protean talents.

Thick skin, anyone?

Some deaf activists argue that we are *not* disabled, that we are a linguistic minority with our own language and culture. Within our own world, filled with phone lights, crybaby lights, closed-caption decoders, videophones, etc.—perhaps. But we are undeniably shaped by the hearing world.

If the majority culture's main means of communicating information and cultural mores is through sound, then we are disabled. Even though I personally don't see deafness as a disability, I accept the fact that it *is* a disability in the eyes of the general population. For that reason alone, I feel sad about the deaf community's insistence on separating itself from the disabled community.

We should work together because we are not physically perfect and because we need to look beyond labels. This is a palpable threat for many hearing and able-bodied people, because we embody their private fears—in reality. They could be us, and this freaks them out. No wonder why the deaf and disabled aren't exactly popular causes, even with an estimated 25 million Americans with hearing loss problems in this country alone. In fact, I doubt the deaf and disabled rights movements would ever be popular until at least *half* of this country is affected and afflicted on a personal level. Until then it's still going to be sweaty grunge work to get heard.

In the meantime disabled artists have a lot to teach each other, but so do a lot of able-bodied artists. The impulse they share to communicate to their audiences is indeed universal.

71

I still feel irritated by the I. King Jordan quote: "Deaf people can do anything except to hear." Excuse me, but what about Evelyn Glennie, the most famous living percussionist? And some of us deaf people do have some residual hearing and enjoy music as a result.

What's wrong with saying, "Deaf people can do *anything*" and leave our ears out of it?

We can accomplish a great deal more when we stop thinking about the state of our ears all the time.

72

For a long time I didn't know how to describe the discrimination against deaf people with a single term. I knew of racism, xenophobia, and homophobia, but what about us deaf people?

The researcher Tom Humphries has given us such a word: "audism." First invented in the 1970s, audism encompasses discrimination or stereotypes against deaf or hard of hearing people. For example, some audists might assume that the cultural ways of hearing people are preferable or superior to those of deaf or signing culture, or that deaf people are somehow less capable than hearing people, as in the ASL idiom "hearie-think." This meaning has evolved from Dr. Humphries's initial definition of audism as "the notion that one is superior based on one's ability to hear or behave in the manner of one who hears." Most people would assume that the hearing world has made my life difficult. Not always. I have had some deaf non-signers discriminate against me because I had chosen to sign in public. Never mind the fact that I was raised as an oralist until I graduated from high school, or that my speech is still clear enough to be understood by most hearing strangers.

So, yes, some deaf people can be audist against their own kind.

73

Stories of injustice just because of disability can be tiring. I understand that the frustrations are very real and all, but I'm not interested in listening to people whine. I'm more moved by those who refuse to take any more crap from anybody. Besides, they have the more interesting—and often funnier—stories to tell.

Better yet, people who take action usually have the best things happen to them.

74

Many deaf artists are finding it useful to view their work as part of the larger narrative known as "Deafhood," a concept first coined by Paddy Ladd, a deaf British researcher, in his book *Understanding Deaf Culture*. Largely inspired by the civil rights movement spearheaded by African-Americans in the 1960s, he sought lessons in deaf people's history from which the deaf community could benefit. Genie Gertz, a faculty member of the Deaf Studies Department at California State University, Northridge (CSUN), explains Deafhood succinctly in an online ASL video, of which an English translation follows: "Deafhood means a process, a journey for all Deaf people. It is not a measurement who is Deaf and who is not. It is a process of becoming the best Deaf human being one can become. There are two definitions: deafness and deafhood. Deafness is a term often determined by the medical field that focuses on abnormality, diagnosis, and handicap. It also focuses on looking at deaf people as individuals with hearing loss. On the other hand, deafhood is a process, not a state, which focuses on people's existential stances. Their existences strongly tie to normality, collectivism, and recognition of the shared beliefs and values. This is not about labeling one another, not about whether you are a big 'D' or a small 'd.' This is about all of us being deaf with full support of everyone's journey to reach Deafhood. That is to unite us all, not to divide us."

Amen!

75

Even as I rail against the proliferation of hacks, I have to acknowledge that we do need hacks as much as we need artists. We need hacks as a bas relief for the artists—to contrast with how good the artists can be—so we can more fully appreciate the true artist. In other words, hacks make dinner with Tuna Helper and artists make dinner with tuna tartar with the freshest ingredients.

76

If it's just impossible to get a definition of art that everyone can agree on, then what the tarnation is art? Art is always an emotional honesty in search of a question.

77

Art should have boundless passion. It isn't enough that the artist is obsessed with the themes in question; she must be able to make her obsession contagious enough that the only way to cure ourselves is to take her full medicine.

Art should have structure, obvious or not.

The artist knows how to edit and revise and manipulate the work in question for a desired effect at a certain moment; if the artist wishes to produce only first drafts, we'll get another round of mumbo-jumbo that only adds to art's unfairly tainted name.

One of the poet Allen Ginsberg's most quoted dictums is "First thought, best thought." Many writers took this to mean that first drafts were basically worthy and best not tampered with. However, there is plenty of evidence that Ginsberg constantly reworked what became his most famous poem "Howl." The published poem sounds natural and powerful, but comparing the progressive drafts from the first reveals how first thoughts weren't always best. Once he began to believe that dictum too much later in his career, the quality of his work began to decline.

79

Art is truth, factual or not.

No one likes being lied to, which explains partly why some people—while they don't like being lied to—turn their faces away when the truth is much too stark, too overwhelming. Yet we do *respond* when faced with something truthful; when we respond so intensely, it's often a statement of how much deception we have to live with in order to have access to truth.

80

Art is presence. It isn't afraid of being unique. Regardless of how the work in question was achieved, we must experience the full force of the work before us. Each work of art should have its own DNA. We must detect traces of its mixed parentages here and there, but the work in question should be as distinctively different from the artist's creative relatives.

81

Many times, when I'm shopping at my favorite grocery store, I will spot Seventh Generation's cleaning products. The reason why the company chose their name is this Great Law of the Iroquois Confederacy quote: "In our every deliberation, we must consider the impact of our decisions on the next seven generations." Searching online for this exact quote, I discovered something else that must've been cut: ". . . even if it requires having skin as thick as the bark of a pine." How true!

It isn't just the environment we need to care about. We need to think about how our art will affect other generations from now. We have to be willing to let our artwork become a historical record of sorts, and pray that it will inspire others to make this world a better place than the world we left.

82

The most concrete way of seeing what art can do is to look how *deeply* intimate and memorable food can be.

When I lived in New York, my favorite restaurant was Gramercy Tavern, and this is largely because of two cooks who'd worked there at the time: Tom Colicchio, who devised the most amazing meals out of the freshest ingredients from the local farmer's market on Union Square, and Claudia Fleming, who enabled me to appreciate her Coconut Tapioca Soup among her many dessert feats.

Both their spirit of elegant experimentation and quest for freshness is the earmark of true gourmands—they are artists seeking to evolve to the higher power of the tongue. Even though Colicchio and Fleming are no longer at Gramercy Tavern, I've come away with meals that were totally unforgettable yet sated me beyond my stomach. To me, to be able to remember such singular meals out of the thousands I've eaten in my life so far is a testimonial to the sheer presence that only true artists can provide.

83

I'm always in awe of artists who've mastered skills to do what they want most to do. Actors, for instance, enthrall me because I have such terrible memory retention for dialogue; the fact that I write for theater and film doesn't matter. To be able to remember lines *and* to give them an emotional shading that I'd never envisioned originally just awes me; worse yet, to do it night after night in front of a roomful of strangers is astonishing indeed. I pity the actress who must struggle with a badly written part.

84

It isn't enough that a poet reads other people's work. She has to *think* about the poems to which she reacts most strongly.

I don't care if a poem makes me react in a positive or negative manner; the key word here is *strongly*. I want a poem to make me feel *something*. The poet needs to look at her favorite poems by other writers and explore precisely *why* they are her favorites. I'm not saying that she needs to put on her English Literature hat and apply academic theories to her findings.

It is enough to say: "Oh, I really like the way that line alliterates." "The line break right after that word really accentuates the drama in the next line." Little things, but what little things!

A great poem is always filled with little things.

Such is the case with great works of art elsewhere.

The artist must be willing to appreciate the work of those whom she sees as her rivals. She must accept the fact that no matter how accomplished or great her work might be, she'll never be the *only* artist who matters.

86

Within the signing deaf community, all deaf artists are automatically labeled "hearie-think." (This ASL idiom is derived from the sign for "hearing," which is the index finger rotated from sideways in front of your lips; bring the sign up to your forehead where "think" is.) The accuser is often someone who doesn't try to understand art, and therefore, other kinds of people. The otherness of people and their own experiences is what often makes art exciting, and yes, transcendent at times. The deaf artist cannot avoid this label. Accept this reality and move on to what your heart really desires.

87

All reactions to any work in question are valid. Occasionally, the reasons and/or rationalizations for their reactions make me wonder. The artist must be prepared enough for comments like "That looks like crap!" to explore why it looks like crap to that particular person. "You know" doesn't qualify as an answer. You cannot read their minds for the real reasons why. Sometimes people feel intimidated by what you are trying to say in the work in question that they feel compelled to lie (as in "Interesting") in order not to hurt your feelings *and* let themselves off the hook. You must encourage them to share their honest feelings because as an artist, you have an enormous obligation to truth, whatever it may be—emotional, factual, fantastical, or otherwise. The only thing to be learned from a lie is how bitter its aftertaste is.

This is even more difficult when you ask for feedback from a deaf person. There is a deep prejudice against being labeled as a "hearie-think," so naturally some intelligent deaf people hide their real selves until they are alone with whom they see as their peers (who are also in danger of being labeled like them). So, in a way, "hearie-thinkers" are very much in the closet! Obviously, for the deaf artist to thrive, they *must* come out and show their support. Maybe the work in question isn't that great (or strikes them as beyond comprehension), but nevertheless, the deaf artist needs to be encouraged to keep trying.

Some deaf artists are lucky that their audiences don't care at all what the work involves because the artist is deaf, just like them. Output of erratic quality is beside the point. Deaf pride is what counts here. While such unconditional love and acceptance is rare and wonderful, the deaf artist suffers in the long run. The work, because it hasn't been road-tested "out there," becomes increasingly contrived, secondhand. A certain kind of humility is required of every artist in order to create memorable works.

What if a deaf gourmet chef ate only food cooked by other deaf chefs who also eat dishes cooked by other deaf chefs? The true cook-artist would go out there in the world and sample everything, analyze cooking techniques used to achieve certain culinary effects, and so on. The cook-artist is immeasurably enriched by the knowledge she has acquired, and through which she can apply her own vision of cooking to her recipes. Art is not about deaf or hearing; art demands an openness and a willingness to be corrupted in thought and sensibility.

Many people seem to assume that a mediocrity of talent is sufficient to propel anyone to the top. Not so. In this society (well, perhaps in *all* societies!), a little persistence, a little talent, and connections do matter. If the hack succeeds (with a lot of hype and/or money) on her first or second try, those who see themselves as artists much superior to the hack will bemoan the hack's subsequent successes. Naturally, jealousy and resentment run rampant. Pettiness rules. But then again, the hack becomes painfully clichéd past the point of parody. Sometimes it's not fun to watch. The hack being slaughtered beyond reason could be us when we stay up there too long.

Instead of tearing down the hacks who keep usurping your chances at success, channel your anger and jealousy to where it truly matters—your work. In no way am I saying that your work should be angry as you are. However, the energy levels produced by anger can provide unbeatable fuel for the work in progress. Think not of that look of shock and envy on the hack's face but of how much pleasure (and getting beneath their skins) your new work will give. You'd be amazed at how much you can accomplish with constructively-used anger.

Art should be about creation and expression, not competition.

The critic is rightfully the enemy of art. I say this in spite of the fact that I do enjoy reading reviews and have discovered some new voices I wouldn't have found otherwise. (Critics who feel morally responsible in this sense are unfortunately far and few.) Even though critics may not mean to do so, they play right into human nature's need for conformity. If a work of art is deemed worthy, everyone follows *à la* mob psychology, even if the work itself seems dubious in value. This is regrettable because art should be about experiencing something for oneself, and not in the context of about to be categorized/analyzed; thus, our honest responses are automatically compromised.

Art is not theory; art is reperception incarnate.

91

The artist speaks alone, and often passionately for the freedom of self-expression. She knows firsthand, and often humiliatingly so, what it feels like to be told to express herself in a certain way, even if it's totally contrary to her private beliefs. There's a specific reason why censorship in all forms is the one thing the artist detests most about the society she lives in.

Being deaf might strike hearing people as a state of isolation, but not so.

Isolation is a myth.

Just because we are deficient in one sense does not mean that our other remaining senses automatically overcompensate.

Yes, the reality of not hearing everything around us might create unintended rifts between ourselves and the world. Rather, it is more often that people who find it difficult to teach deaf students in the first place may struggle with the notion of exposing their students to all kinds of art, and expect genuine appreciation in return. To them it seems like a waste of time. These people have already given up on the slim possibility of their deaf students ever developing an artistic sensibility that could enable them to appreciate and enjoy the finer things in life. I think this explains partly why there aren't more deaf people who are attuned to what artists—deaf or hearing—have to say.

93

Quite a few people have speculated that when one of our five senses fails, we compensate more perceptually with our remaining senses. In this case, many have believed that our sense of sight is heightened because we are forced to pay more attention to our surroundings. Nothing could be further from the truth.

I have found that many deaf people, especially when they do not rely on their hearing aids as much, find learning ASL to be far easier. The language of hands itself has spatial relationships and visual information that most people never think about until they subconsciously begin to break down such elements during the act of signing. Thus each sign becomes a photograph of sorts, a constant clicking of what we are simultaneously seeing *and* sharing with another person. We see the size of a building or the length between two landmarks, and automatically scale such measurement proportionately. We do this without much thought; we've had a lifetime of observing a little longer than most people. We simply record what we see and forget about what we've just seen. Our brains become super-fast hard drives with each image already broken down into smaller parts, each a file of its own that we call upon when we want to convey something with our hands.

We have within the miracle of our hands a constant carousel of slides projected rather like holograms in thin air. Even if we may have never studied the history and aesthetics of fine art photography, we possess an unerring instinct of what works visually. We live and breathe in the photography of language itself.

Art should provoke one into motion (and emotion). Art should never be so neutral that we can simply go on to the next thing as if nothing's happened. Art should grab our attention and hold it long enough to reveal slowly its riches, as if time is a wind pushing the smoke of our first impressions away. It exists to challenge. When we feel challenged by all our frustrations, we feel most alive.

Art should remind us what it means to live, to feel, to remember. Otherwise, it's too long a journey from cradle to grave.

95

Artists by their very nature are often eccentric and quirky. They should be. Living one's art means striking out on one's own and finding new paths in uncharted woods. It means that their husbands, wives, lovers, and partners must often make sacrifices for the muse, whom they meet under countless disguises in their loved one's work. Sometimes they resent the power the muse has, but then again, they often can't *hate*, as the muse has shaped their loved one long before they'd met.

I dislike the label "genius." For one thing, the word has been overused that it's become rather meaningless. The term should never be applied to a living artist; only time would tell whether the living artist's work will survive her death. Artists are egomaniacs at heart, which comes from having enough nerve to share their nakedness in a world filled with automatic rejection. No need to make them think they're better than what they really are.

Labels simply make it harder for the artist to be more honest with herself.

97

The impulse to create requires a small ego; children create as a matter of course. But to expect to be a professional creator of some sort requires a bigger ego. How else can they combat that consuming fear of being ridiculed and laughed at? The artist has to feel confident enough to make that first statement in the first of many attempts at a clearer self-expression.

Everyone has an inner artist waiting to come out. The fear of being belittled has too often swallowed their keys to artistic freedom.

When I talk about art in general, I refer also to disciplines not traditionally thought of as being artistic. Automobile mechanics have an intuitive understanding of how different cars operate under different conditions; troubleshooting is often more than rocket science. Physicists and astronomers are always looking for an elegance in order and labeling, so the ever-expanding universe can't overwhelm the human mind—yet. And even my own dentist intuitively understands where pain is in any part of my teeth; he is able to provide suggestions to ease the pain as he operates on my toothache. When it comes to medical science, knowledge and experience may seem to be everything, but I disagree—a genuine caring for the patient's needs is nearly a lost art.

Artists should never be so intellectual that they forget all about their baser instincts. Gore Vidal once said that theater audiences—well, he could've been talking about *any* audience!—are interested in three things: Sex, death, and money, in that order. We are deeply affected by all three in our own lives, so naturally, we are interested in how others cope.

Art is coping, and I'm not talking about art-is-therapy crap! More precisely, art is struggle aching for immortality.

100

Accessibility in workshops—I'm talking about creative writing workshops here—creates a real problem for the deaf artist wishing to be true to herself. While the interpreter may be invaluable for making the classroom discussion clear and easier to follow, I find that for those hearing colleagues and peers of the deaf artist, the interpreter is seen as a barrier to communication. How can the hearing colleague feel encouraged to communicate on an honest level with the deaf artist? The fact that all interpreters are bound by their code of ethics, in which client confidentiality is paramount, doesn't matter. The more people are involved with an exchange, the harder it is to be totally honest, as the fear of being judged and rebuked increases proportionately by the number of people involved. I feel this situation acutely when I give readings from my own work: When I sign with an interpreter voicing for me, the number of hearing readers wishing me to autograph their books dwindles to almost zero; however, if I use my voice at some point in public, the number of hearing readers eager to meet with me after the reading shoots straight up. Hearing people still equate speech to communication when communication is far more than the sum of voice and ear.

Hearing people have a long way to go in their understanding of what communication truly means.

And art has the potential power of rendering the mere act of communication meaningless.

101

When artists become considered part of a classifiable movement—or an easily recognizable iconography—it quickly becomes a marketing thing. "Oh, Monet is an Impressionist painter. Water lilies, haystacks, stuff like that." "Georgia O'Keeffe painted close-ups of bones." "Picasso does that Cubist thing, right?" And so on. Hearing artists were always recognized.

But deaf artists? Not many were acknowledged. Some felt that there needed to be a formal statement about deaf art. In May 1989, nine deaf people with a vested interest in art came up with a manifesto.

The De'VIA Manifesto
Deaf View/Image Art

De'VIA represents Deaf artists and perceptions based on their Deaf experiences. It uses formal art elements with the intention of expressing innate cultural or physical Deaf experience. These experiences may include Deaf metaphors, Deaf perspectives, and Deaf insight in relationship with the environment (both the natural world and Deaf cultural environment), spiritual and everyday life.

De'VIA can be identified by formal elements such as Deaf artists' possible tendency to use contrasting colors and values, intense colors, contrasting textures. It may also most often include a centralized focus, with exaggeration or emphasis on facial features, especially eyes, mouths, ears, and hands. Currently, Deaf artists tend to work in human scale with these exaggerations, and not exaggerate the space around these elements.

There is a difference between Deaf artists and De'VIA. Deaf artists are those who use art in any form, media, or subject matter, and who are held to the same artistic standards as other artists. De'VIA is created when the artist intends to express their Deaf experience through visual art. De'VIA may also be created by deafened or hearing artists, if the intention is to create work that is born of their Deaf experience (a possible example would be a hearing child of Deaf parents). It is clearly possible for Deaf artists not to work in the area of De'VIA.

While applied and decorative arts may also use the qualities of De'VIA (high contrast, centralized focus, exaggeration of specific features), this manifesto is specifically written to cover the traditional fields of visual fine arts (painting, sculpture, drawing, photography, printmaking) as well as alternative media when used as fine arts such as fiber arts, ceramics, neon, and collage.

As historically important as this document is, it's my hope that we deaf artists won't feel bound by the expectations set forth here and that we will use our work to create manifestos all our own.

102

The most terrifying thing about being a deaf artist is the fact that you are constantly trying to find your own place in the world that won't stay still long enough for you to get your bearings. You know you are deaf, but you are too "hearie-think" to fit in completely with the deaf community. You know you are "hearie-think" but you are too deaf to fit in comfortably with the world of your hearing artistic community.

Making your own homestead on a new frontier is always difficult. Right now the deaf artist is very much a pioneer, which affords her truly extraordinary opportunities to make a difference in the most unexpected ways.

103

Art must come at you from sideways. It should happen to you so quickly that you may feel ticked off at being caught unawares. Art should unsettle your senses enough so that you should remember never to take the abundance of life for granted. That is also the genuine value of shock—beyond that is mere sensationalism, often for hype and profit.

Art is pornography of the highest order—it stimulates all our intellectual, emotional, and spiritual organs in spite of ourselves.

I sometimes feel art can be like pornography because in today's world, it occasionally feels obscene to feel anything.

104

Art should elevate you and drag you down at the same time. Which is what life usually does. Art reflects life. In fact, for the artist, there is usually no separation between her life and art. Life and art constantly feed off each other. The artist is a complete synergistic creature. The how is not as important as the what she is trying to say.

105

After a certain point in her life, the artist should feel self-confident enough to discard those bouts of insecurity and jealousy of other artists who are making it to the big time, whatever that means. The artist must learn to live with the frustrating contention that her time will come. But often, as the cliché goes, all good things do come to all those who wait. To that, I'd add more to those who continue to work at their craft during their long wait.

106

Many artists go mad partly because not enough people around them seem to appreciate their work. By the same token, it's amazing that more deaf people haven't gone mad, as the hearing world isn't always understanding of them. Perhaps deaf people are better suited to be artists more than they realize. Being understood by hearing people has always taken time, so patience and clarity are traits cherished in deaf culture.

107

Some people are initially attracted to the idea of being artists because so many of the celebrated artists seem to have all the girls (or boys) plus fame and fortune. While this in itself isn't necessarily a bad thing, many artists quickly find such initial impulses to be shallow. This weeds out the worst of the hacks, but never enough, of course.

Thus the artist's motivation for staying committed to her craft becomes deeper, richer, and more meaningful. These new reasons often shine through her work, intentionally or not.

108

The artist does not necessarily have to suffer and starve for her work. I believe that it is possible to find a full-time (or part-time) day job that would enable the ease of financial stability so that she can otherwise afford to explore her creative energies without worrying so much about money and bills. The series of my dead-end jobs, while frustrating at times, was fantastic for my needs as an artist: I didn't have to take the job home with me, I got annual salary raises, and everyone understood why I continued to stay on even when I was obviously overqualified for my job. My dead-end jobs were only steppingstones to bigger things as an artist.

109

When one chooses to become an artist, mere crass commercialism becomes no longer a livable option. It is good, however, to be aware of what sells, and what all the trends are. But do not let these flavor-of-the-month trends sway you from listening to your own muse. When you ignore all those trends and listen only to yourself, it's very possible that your own work will spark a trend all its own at the right time.

The true artist sets trends without expecting to; she will quickly move on to something else, or suffer the curse of being too closely identified with a faddish movement that she had no intention of starting in the first place. The artist will always want something different, and she must pray that her audiences will be as ready for something different. When the world is ready for something different as she is, a new "trend" is born right there on the spot.

110

I know a few poets who are embittered because they feel they didn't get the recognition they felt were owed to them. I've tried to explain that *everyone*—artists or not—often feels that way, and how important it is to let that bitterness go. Many awarded poets don't get read after they're dead, and many poets who never won major awards while alive do get widely read after they're gone.

We artists don't get much of a say in how our work will be accepted. The most important thing is to live in the moment and celebrate both the static and the ecstatic in our work.

111

Rejection is the hallmark of every artist's life.

Accept praise when it finally comes, but do not let it go to your head. The next rebuff is coming at you faster than you think!

112

Self-righteousness does not suit the artist very well. The artist has enough bad PR as it is. There must be enough humility left in the artist to allow her to see how she could constantly improve her craft.

113

The artist has an obligation to support the small and independent businesses in her community. Running a small business with any sort of profitability is an art into itself. Moreover, as in the case of independent bookstores and art galleries, the managers understand the meaning of independence in a world that's increasingly monolithic and corporate.

It is through the artist that our hopes for a greater humanity exist. She brings our needs and desires home in a way that economic justification can't. It isn't enough to say that we are suffering; it's far better to show *how* we are suffering.

Hacks tell; artists show.

The hack tries to please everyone. The artist tries to please a select few, namely herself above all in the name of emotional resonance. That is the basic difference between hacks and artists—that is, instant quantity and long-lasting quality.

114

As an artist, I made a very conscious choice *not* to have children. I knew that as much as I'd love my own children, I'd be forever frustrated with familial responsibility getting in the way of the time I need for my craft. I am always in awe of artists who are able to juggle their creative impulses with their parental duties.

For me, having a dog provides the breaks I require every once in a while. Walking my dog Rocky around the neighborhood or taking a quick nap with my head resting on his pillowy back on the floor often refreshes me enough to go back to work with a revitalized perspective. That's why I sometimes jokingly call Rocky my "office assistant."

115

From the hearing perspective, deafness more than any other disability strikes at the heart of communication, which is speech-oriented. The fear of never hearing music again, which most hearing people love and take for granted, is akin for some to losing their ability to walk again. The fear—and the fascination—is what attracts many hearing people to the deaf community. Of course, doctors, scientists, and researchers want to eradicate that fear of hearing loss for once and for all with a variety of medical and technological breakthroughs, the most notorious being the cochlear implant.

Even if deafness may be eradicated completely over the next century, we are going to crave and imagine the experience of being deaf. It is so obvious a metaphor that is waiting to be explored in the future: Is it really better and humane to be physically perfect that we begin to forget that imperfection has shaped what we are now? Deafness will always intrigue artists because it seems such an obvious barrier to what they want to excel in: communication.

The irony is that the world itself is a far bigger barrier than most people realize.

116

The artist's physical disability is never a handicap. Rather, the artist's reception to new ideas and approaches that run contrary to her own is the bigger obstacle to her craft. The more closed-minded she is, the more the vitality of her craft sags.

117

Art should never be pure; art should always be corrupted. In this day and age, it is impossible to make it pure. You should try creating something in a new medium, and then switch back to the medium of your choice.

A different perspective is often very helpful in developing and mastering your craft. When I am writing a play, I often like to read novels and essays. If I'm writing fiction, I love to read poetry, and pay close attention to how actors—great or not—choose to behave on stage and screen.

It helps to think "cross-platform" when working on something new.

118

Art demands translation.

Translation, when it comes to art, has nothing to do with signed, spoken, or written languages. Yes, there are facts that we may need to know, but when we see a work of art so totally foreign to our way of thinking, we are stuck unless we choose to interpret.

We need to feel, on a gut level, that our efforts to try understanding it will be rewarded with a greater understanding of the world and ourselves.

However subtle its beckoning it may be, it must first invite us in.

James Joyce's *Dubliners* is a great collection of short stories about a certain point in time, ending with "The Dead," which many consider to be *the* greatest short story ever written in English.

But his novel *Ulysses* seems wholly arcane and inaccessible at first. Once you understand that it is Joyce's *interpretation* of Ulysses's journey home from fighting the Trojan War for so many years reimagined as one day of the advertising salesman Leopold Bloom's life on June 16, 1904 in Dublin, the story invites us to rethink many of our associations we've made with language.

As deaf artists, we are naturally sensitive to all aspects of communication. We feel the pain of misunderstanding far more than what most hearing people realize. We often suffer because it is usually too late to rectify because the misunderstanding has snowballed into something too big for us to fix.

Art is undiluted communication diluted from experience.

RAYMOND LUCZAK

Because many deaf people transverse the trapeze rope between English and ASL, they are naturally concerned with the finer points of translation.

Some twenty years ago I worked with Clayton Valli, the ASL poet, on translating his poem "A Dandelion" into English:

Their yellows dotted the field,
their petals waving with the breezes.

An irritated man stared at them, snarling,
"Dandelions!" His hands pulled
some apart, and mowed the rest down
until the field was smoothed out
in green. The rain soon came
and went away; the sun sneaked in,
warming a seed in the soil.
The seed rose, enjoying all nature.

It waved, watching a bee
coming by with a greeting and
going away. Nights it closed
its petals, opening up again
in the morning. One day it turned
into white puffs, their whiskers
a halo, but it still moved with the breeze.
Its seedlings flew off in every direction.

Spotting its whiteness, the man,
enraged, spit out, "There!"
The brave white puff still waved,

still sending off its seedlings.
The man grabbed its stem and pulled out.
The white puff exploded, its seedlings
scattering everywhere on its own.

In my translation, it's a story poem. It has a beginning, a middle, and an end.

I chose to tell its story rather than to focus on corresponding the hand-rhyming schemes with its English equivalents, the repetition of certain handshapes, and other elements that comprise the full body of his ASL poem. How does one convey the full majesty of his poem on paper other than to see it with her own eyes? No one can.

A great deal is lost in translation of an ASL poem, only because paper is the worst place for such attempts.

But "A Dandelion" remains pure dynamite in Valli's hands, in his unfettered and yet controlled ASL; it also happens to be my favorite ASL poem because it means so much to *me*. It is hard not to recall how often ASL has been the traditional target of those in deaf education who've seen ASL detrimental to deaf children learning English, and yet it is moving to realize that ASL will survive like the dandelion no matter how hard the medical profession wishes to wipe out deafness. At least that is my interpretation of his poem "A Dandelion."

Another person could see the dandelion as a symbol of another minority's culture facing extinction; another could see it as a comical story of a meticulous man wanting to keep his lawn weed-free.

Art is our fountain of youth, for as long as we explore it, we keep alive our wondrous curiosity.

120

So: What's the difference between "translation" and "interpretation"?

Translation, for me, is an attempt to get the facts embedded in the work itself into another language.

Interpretation is an attempt to articulate my personal views about the work after experiencing the work itself.

The reader can fault my translation for being too loose, or too literal, if she already knows ASL, sees Valli's poem in person (or on video), and reads my translation. That would be *her* interpretation of my translation, and not of the ASL poem itself.

However flawed my translation of Valli's poem may be, it is my hope that the translation itself will entice readers to want to dive into the beautiful night-lit shimmering swimming pool that is ASL itself.

Better yet, have them want to become ASL poets and storytellers themselves!

121

ASL is more than fingers that paint.

It is more than eyebrows asking a question.

It is more than movement that tell stories.

It is more than hands that sing.

It is more than people who can't speak clearly.

In a world that tells us it's impossible to dream of big things and not have our hearts broken, ASL remains the mother lode of dreams. Among ourselves we can dare to dream recklessly in a language so calmly clear as sun and moon, and perhaps find a new-lighted way to something bigger than any of us has ever imagined.

Before ASL, I was a dreamer afraid to share because it wasn't always easy to speak, especially when I had a large vocabulary most of which I'd never heard pronounced. I sat there in my hearing classroom, wondering when I would get to spread my wings and fly. It'd never occurred to me in those days that the power to fly was already in my hands.

When I came to Gallaudet and discovered a campus filled with signing everywhere I went, I found myself uncaged. Suddenly I could share my hopes and my past.

ASL gave me the passport to soar and dream.

And in art, there are so many wonderful countries to explore.

122

Art is interpretation.

What the artist does for us is to *interpret* her own experiences in a meaningful way to her, and in a way that also enables us to understand and appreciate her point of view.

123

Art requires interpretation, at least enough to make it personal for each one of us. When we decide this or that person's work is not worth our time, the decision is rarely made randomly; it is the final decision made from a series of smaller decisions which outcomes have rewarded—or hurt—us.

If I am put off by the work of Salvador Dalí, the ubër-Surrealist artist of the 20th century, there's a good chance that I may not like René Magritte's work, which is sort of like Surrealism but not as in-your-face.

But if I love both Martin Scorsese's and Robert Altman's work as filmmakers, there's a good chance I will gravitate toward Paul Thomas Anderson's work.

Art begets art.

124

As the means of transmitting art to the masses become increasingly digital, the biggest threat to the artist is the distributor. In order to get her books bought and read, the writer must deal with the distributor, who can then make sure her titles are available once they are reviewed. The same thing goes for the musician who releases her work. Even the painter must go to a gallery owner/representative, a nicer-sounding name for a distributor. But what about marketing? It's become far more important than anything.

The Internet is the first global market square where everyone from every single country has the potential to mingle and learn from each other without the need for a passport. In that sense, the user-friendly accessibility to the Internet may be the *one* technological event with the most impact on the artist herself since the advent and affordability of the home computer. Art is without borders, and the Internet does not recognize borders. Creativity, an open mind, and a little patience are every artist's passport online.

But an online presence shouldn't be everything to the artist starting out.

People are still very tactile-oriented. Even though I have ordered books online, I still prefer to browse books with my hands. I have a concrete sense of its weight, its writing style, its artwork, and so on—subjective things that no one can experience for me.

125

Art should withstand the ravages of time. It should sustain itself regardless of the epoch we live in. Even though the story takes place in the 1940s, the film *It's A Wonderful Life* is absolutely timeless. Its themes of redemption through the love of family and friends are so potent that even I, who can be cynical and jaded at times, am brought to tears at the film's epiphanic end. It doesn't matter that I may've seen the film five times already. It *endures*.

Such is the power of art that seeks to redeem.

126

The one sign idiom I wish was never invented is this: "hearie-think." The sign for "hearing" is a tiny circle spinning forward and made at the chin to indicate a person speaking. The idiom "hearie-think" is the same sign for "hearing" but brought up to the forehead to mean that the person thinks—or wants to be—like a hearing person.

It is an incredibly powerful idiom that diminishes the potential interest of the deaf community in the artist's work.

Labels have been known to hurt and afflict many people, but this one label has frightened away so many potential deaf artists who are otherwise seeking acceptance from their "friends." I say "friends" because true friends will accept you as you are.

127

Disability is not the only obstacle that the budding deaf artist faces.

Class is more of a barrier, I think, because if you dress well (or better) due to a nice allowance from your parents or a hefty credit card, the sign idiom "hearie-think" is awfully close to the sign for "stuck-up." (In fact, that was how I came to write *Snooty*—instead of trying to explain that peculiar idiom to hearing audiences who'd know nothing about deaf culture, I used a concept that seems to be, unfortunately, universal.) I have had people turn me down or move away because I didn't look "right" fashion-wise.

128

Art should reflect the tumult of the times we live in. The work should be hybrid in nature but pure in impulse. Every day we deal with the extremes of wanting to cling to old-fashioned values in an age that insists we let go of our traditional ways.

The artist should be obsessed with these kinds of traditions: the past, the present, and the future. She is omniscient in impulse, acts as if she is Goddess, and then allows herself to fall down to the earth with her audience.

To survive as an artist, she must both embrace and ignore all extremes.

129

Bitterness is a very unbecoming quality for the artist.

So is backstabbing, as in "hearie-think."

Try not to be bitter. It may be a very difficult thing to do, but it's really better for your growing reputation that you do.

130

The artist sees beneath the surface.

Albert Einstein may be referenced as a great example of "genius," but I prefer to think of him as an artist. He saw through facts, assumptions, and theories of his time to conjure a staggering vision so true that in its peak of beauty, it gave mankind the means to create the most lethal weapon of mass destruction: the atomic bomb. I am sure that he was equally horrified that his vision of the universe could unleash so much pain and death.

131

Why create in the first place?

To remember, and to leave behind a record so that others can learn to remember something of what we, now dead, have experienced.

With our ubiquitous digital cameras embedded in our cell phones, we have become photographers of record.

Affordable digital cameras have made it possible for the masses to snap as many pictures as they could possibly want without worrying about the traditionally exorbitant cost of film development. And when PageMaker, the first desktop publishing program, was released for the Macintosh computer in 1985, the little guy felt like a bona-fide publisher, even if it was just a newsletter. Desktop publishing practically obliterated the cobbled-together DIY sensibility of mimeographs and photocopies in favor of something comparable to the output from graphic design, advertising, and publishing firms. Of course, this tool in the hands of many led to a glut of newsletters and flyers that were immediate eyesores because too many typefaces were used together on the same page. Yet once the euphoria wore off, the fledgling desktop publisher began to appreciate the art and craftsmanship required to create an eye-pleasing page.

Today more people value good graphic design and layout because they've tried to pull off the same thing on their computers. They realize the truly professional work isn't just mastery of a software program or the lighting setups for a well-composed shot: a keen understanding of art as implicit statement.

132

Even though movies try to convince us otherwise when we enter its color-filled dreams, it is believed that we dream only in black and white. This is perhaps why we continue to respond strongly to certain images in monochromatic shades of black and white.

A mysterious image can suggest enough to trigger that something from deep inside our hypothalamus, that special place in our brains that fires off chemicals to which we respond with various emotions. Many times we cannot articulate those fleeting thoughts, but we are often enormously affected. Why else could we find ourselves occasionally stopping to think of someone we'd forgotten twenty years before while standing amidst the blue brightness of a window cleaner waiting to be taken off the shelves and put into a shopping cart? Logic has no place in memory or in dreams.

Sometimes, in the deconstruction of an artwork, the original magic dissipates. We are left with a feeling of desolation. *Was that all? I thought I'd felt so much more than that.* This is why reading art criticism can be a dangerous act for those wishing to appreciate art on a gut level; no one should have to feel that they're supposed to feel certain emotions or "get" something from the artwork. I much prefer to experience a work of art in all its glory, to *see* it not with just my eyes, but with my blind heart that can respond before I can. When I catch up with my heart, I know something has happened, however insignificant. I must open my eyes and *look* again.

133

A work of art should be a celebration of sorts. It shouldn't be *so* casual, or it will have lost its sense of ritual. As much as I bemoan homophobia as an unfortunate aftereffect of Western religious dogma, and as much as I call myself a "recovering Catholic," I do miss rituals. There was something very indelible about attending Mass, which rarely varied on Sundays, that I never got to appreciate until three decades later. I still don't believe in Western religions, especially when so many of its practitioners have too often confused it with spirituality. I see every art gallery and museum as religious shrines to honesty of intent and expression.

I worship art. I believe that each artist is a goddess in her own right, especially if the work in question becomes as powerful as a calling to a higher purpose, a constant questioning of faith. Should I believe what I am experiencing? Why should I believe? Each work of art could be seen as a commandment, a moral lesson more powerful than a prayer uttered out of rote. A great work of art isn't just an excuse to think and analyze so that one can sound erudite; it must convey *emotion*, the very stuff that we human beings are made of.

Art offers redemption, but not quite what others might expect. Unexpected discoveries are what prod us forward in our greater understanding of ourselves.

134

A snapshot is just that, a snap judgment of randomness.

But when one takes the time to plot a narrative of some kind within the narrow confines of a single shot, the image can linger in a person's mind long after the initial viewing. Here, like all great works that many artisans pride on their apparent sleight-of-handedness, is the minimal combination of image and symbol and mood to produce a maximum of impact.

Leonardo da Vinci's *La Gioconda (Mona Lisa)* has been celebrated as the most famous work of art; whether it is the greatest work of Western art produced is always up for a lively debate. But most people do not seem aware of this oil painting's extraordinary technique: He had perfected the technique known as *sfumato*, which in Italian means "vanished or evaporated." He was extremely careful to blend everything, layering between colors, so that the woman sitting in front of us was truly lifelike. (Da Vinci worked on the painting on and off from 1503 until shortly before his death in 1519.) The traditional brushstroke on the canvas seemed obliterated; the layers—some as many as 30!—painted of her skin were only a few molecules thick. The first art historians were stunned by how close to flesh and blood she appeared.

Painting is always a time-consuming process, especially when dealing with oil. Da Vinci was a perfectionist in this regard, but aside from the parodies that have made the painting most famous from the 19th century and on, the painting is still memorable and has become a part of our *lingua franca* when talking about art. Despite the stunning infrared photographs of Da Vinci's hidden layers revealing his original intents (who knew that *Mona Lisa* originally wore a bonnet?), he framed a mysterious narrative that continue to engage us more than half a millennia later.

Not many painters use *sfumato* in their work these days, but I like to think that *sfumato* has been redefined altogether by a whole new generation of digital artists. Photoshop, the leading image manipulation program, uses the concept of layers in the same way, forcing its users to break down each element of the image so that the overall vision appears believable even though reality may dictate otherwise. Manipulation is one thing, but having something compelling to convey without calling too much attention to its own special effects (e.g., effects for effects' sake) is a whole other matter.

That is what great works of art—regardless of tools used—should aim to do, to keep all of us in a state of constant engagement over what it means to be human, and where we are headed next.

135

When it comes to how deaf people dream, I've been asked questions like: "How do you dream? Do you 'hear' yourself as hearing people can? Do you sign in ASL or use spoken English?"

I've wondered for years why such questions irked me so. Yes, there was the obvious idea that if one loses her hearing, she must dream differently. I honestly don't know because I don't recall my dreams involving sound. Yet I have just enough residual hearing to appreciate songs by many pop and rock acts on my iPod, so music must play a part somewhere in my dreams. I simply do not remember it, or maybe sound is simply not as important.

No deaf person ever asks a hearing person: "How do *you* dream?" Minorities do not question the majority's authority enough, which is why deaf artists are far more essential than one might suppose. The view from below is the future mirror of the view from above.

Art should not be dogma; it is only a path toward a greater enlightenment—or perhaps even spirituality—of what we are.

136

Dreaming is a peculiar art. It has its own rules and logic that make no sense whatsoever, but as long as the dreamer puts up no resistance, it is far more potent and oddly meaningful than the best that Old Hollywood could ever have offered. Dreams bypass our first attempts at language, and therefore far more powerful.

Art can wield the same kind of power when we are least prepared for it. The question is: Are we strong and daring enough to dream in ways not our own?

137

Art demands the bravery to try new approaches: Being means sensing, listening, smelling, touching, reading, and closing one's eyes to find a new place that is yours and yours alone.

Be radical every time you start something new. Sometimes you will fail. That's perfectly okay.

You are not a cliché. You will eventually find a solution that works.

Art is a problem with a million solutions waiting to be road-tested. You draw your own map; you are your own cartographer.

It is *your* journey, and no one else's.

138

Deafness—or anything that makes you different—is beautiful.

Do not let anyone tell you otherwise.

If they continue to lie, they do not believe that life itself is beautiful. They want you to be more like them, not to have you be more like *you*.

They are gasping out of rage at their slow and miserable deaths. They can't stand the dull grayness of their limp dreams, let alone comprehend how colorful and self-fulfilling their lives could be.

You are more than *one* color. You are a rainbow bursting at the seams.

Anything that can make you more unique is fantastic and beautiful. We are not automatons; we are *people* with hearts, brains, and lungs; we have souls that yearn to break free and revel in the joy of life's creation. We are all artists seeking colorful expression.

Do not be afraid of the labels slapped on you. Let your heart shrug them off, for labels are only skin-deep, and move on. Yes: *Move on.*

People might sum up my biography thus far: I am an ex-Catholic deaf gay Polish-American writer raised in a hearing family of nine children, and from a small mining town in Michigan's Upper Peninsula.

But I don't see myself that way at all.

I'm only a dreamer seeking to love more of life itself. And art enables me to embrace the world.

In my heart there is no difference between art and deafness.

They are one and the same, for they are both beautiful.

x

RAYMOND LUCZAK

139

Silence is a four-letter word.

Many hearing writers and artists equate deafness with silence of the worst kind—as if never hearing music is the worst thing that could possibly happen. It is a very selfish perspective, never taking into account that many deaf people have led full and rich lives without ever feeling the need to appreciate music the way that hearing people do.

Some ill-informed reporters and writers still use the outdated term "deaf-mute" to describe a signing deaf person, but another offensive term to use in a title of a work related to deafness is "silence" and its variants. I chose to subvert that no-no into a title that the deaf community would understand and appreciate, because art can be a gleeful act of subversion.

But the reality is that deaf artists can no longer be mute with their work. What they have to say is equally important to anyone else's out there, and what they have to say should be cranked up to maximum volume. No listening assistance device needed.

After generations of being measured with decibels, it is time to set fire to all the tiresome metaphors and symbolisms that deaf characters have been trapped in.

I challenge all artists to find new metaphors for deafness and disability. Actually, there shouldn't be any. If the deaf character is as human as everyone else in the story, metaphors and symbolism aren't needed.

When that happens, art can be a powerful tool for social change. Art is the best way to change the world as we know it. Our hearts are the best ears we have.

ABOUT THE AUTHOR

Raymond Luczak grew up in Ironwood and Houghton, Michigan, in a family of nine children, in which he was number seven and the only one deaf. After graduating from high school, he attended Gallaudet University in Washington, D.C., where he earned a B.A. in English. A few months later he moved to New York City, where he would live for seventeen years. It was there that he began creating the first of his fifteen books. Titles include *Road Work Ahead* (Sibling Rivalry Press), *Mute* (A Midsummer Night's Press), and *Assembly Required: Notes from a Deaf Gay Life* (RID Press). His novel *Men with Their Hands* (Queer Mojo) won first place in the Project: QueerLit 2006 Contest.

In addition to working with the acclaimed storyteller Mario Hernandez for the DVD *Manny ASL: Stories in American Sign Language*, he directed and edited the full-length documentaries *Guy Wonder: Stories & Artwork* and *Nathie: No Hand-Me-Downs*. He is also a playwright with nineteen plays performed in three countries.

In 2005, he relocated to Minneapolis, Minnesota. Sibling Rivalry Press will publish his fifth collection of poems *How to Kill Poetry* in the spring of 2013.

www.raymondluczak.com